LONDON BOROUGH OF SOUTHWARK
ADULT LIBRARIES

This is due for return on or before the latest date
marked below. A charge will be made if it is retained for
a longer period. Books may be renewed if not required
by another reader. Not more than two such renewals
may be made by post or telephone and the latest date
and the book number must be quoted.

Opening hours are displayed in the library.

Boogie, Marches, & Ragtime

Edited and arranged for easy piano by
Frank Metis

Foreword

The German philosopher Goethe once wrote, "If I accept you as you are, I will make you worse; however, if I treat you as though you are what you are capable of becoming, I will help you become that." Accordingly, I have designed this series of publications to help you grow as a musician, and to enhance your playing skills as well as broaden your musical horizons. To help you along this path, I have included within these pages various degrees of "easy" arrangements and compositions, together with entertaining, informative, and witty comments and quotations.

To encourage you to pianistically "go public," pages 28 through 31 include a special Recital Solo. Practice it, and you will surely please your family and friends—and garner some well-deserved applause. To further your creative skills, complete the exercise in the Creative Corner on page 32. It's fun to do, and you'll be on the road to writing your own music! Above all, don't be apologetic about being an "amateur musician" or "butterfingers pianist." All artists begin as students—and the great ones remain students! With perseverance, you can attain the musical heights to which you aspire. There is an inspiring story about Benny Goodman, the great jazz clarinetist, and Frank Sinatra, the legendary pop singer. Many years ago, they appeared together in the old Paramount Theater in New York City. Early one morning, Sinatra arrived at the theater and heard Goodman practicing furiously in the basement. "I don't understand you, Benny," he said to Goodman. "You play so great, why do you practice so hard?" Goodman looked at him coldly and replied, "If I didn't practice, I'd only be good!" Take a lesson from Benny—and some of your own musical favorites: All the great ones practice constantly and learn continually—and all of them started off with "easy" folios like this one! I want to express profound appreciation to my outstanding editor Peter Pickow for his assistance in putting these publications together, conceptually and musically. His enormous knowledge and insightful suggestions, always rendered with unfailing courtesy and good humor, managed to track all of my "unguided missiles" and rescue me from foolish ideas. Also, a hug to my son Gregg Metis for coming up with the title for this series.

It has been said that "music washes away from the soul the dust of everyday life." I hope that these pages will help you to do just that. And, may you enjoy having these selections "at your fingertips."

Contents

Front cover illustration: Great Balls O' Fire by Gil Mayers

This book Copyright © 1996 Amsco Publications,
A Division of Music Sales Corporation, New York

Order No. AM 92884
US International Standard Book Number: 0.8256.1463.5
UK International Standard Book Number: 0.7119.4959.X

Exclusive Distributors:
Music Sales Corporation
257 Park Avenue South, New York, NY 10010 USA
Music Sales Limited
8/9 Frith Street, London W1V 5TZ England
Music Sales Pty. Limited
120 Rothschild Avenue, Rosebery, Sydney, NSW 2018 Australia

Printed in the United States of America by
Vicks Lithograph and Printing Corporation

Basic Boogie

by Frank Metis

3

Song: The licensed medium for bawling in
public things too silly or sacred to be uttered
in ordinary speech.

Oliver Herford

Living a Ragtime Life

by Roberts - Jefferson

> *When I hear music, I fear no danger. I am*
> *invulnerable. I see no foe. I am related to the*
> *earliest times and to the latest.*
>   Henry David Thoreau

The Battle of Jericho

Traditional

Josh-ua fit the bat-tle of ___ Jer-i - cho, ___ Jer-i - cho, ___

Jer-i - cho. _____ Josh-ua fit the bat-tle of ___ Jer-i - cho, _ And the

Music produces a kind of pleasure
which human nature cannot do without.
Confucius

Black and White Rag

by George Botsford

When in doubt, sing loud.
Robert Merrill

Bill Bailey, Won't You Please Come Home?

Words and Music by Hughie Cannon

won't you come home?" She cried the

whole night long. "I'll do the dish - es, hon - ey, I'll pay the

rent. I know I done you wrong. 'Mem - ber that

rain - y eve - ning I drove you out with
noth - ing but a fine - tooth comb?
I know I'm to blame, Well,
ain't that a shame? Bill Bai - ley, won't you
please come home?"

Weeping Willow

Moderately slow

by Scott Joplin

13

I only know two tunes; one of them is
"Yankee Doodle" and the other isn't.
Ulysses S. Grant

Yankee Doodle

Traditional

*Any composer's writing is the sum of
himself, of all his roots and influences.*
Leonard Bernstein

The Entertainer

by Scott Joplin

Not too fast

18

Prayer Parade

by Frank Metis

The spirit of music is great enough to include all of us,
whether scholars, composers, clowns or vagabond minstrels.

Walter Starkie

Broadway Parade

by Frank Metis

A careless song, with a little nonsense in it
now and then, does not misbecome a monarch.
Horace Walpole

Ballin' the Jack Boogie

Moderately, with a steady beat

Words by James Henry Burris
Music by Chris Smith

First you put your two knees close up tight, __ Then you sway 'em to the left, then you sway 'em to the right, Step a-round the floor kind of nice and light, __ Then you

*Music is in the air–you simply
take as much of it as you want.*
Sir Edward Elgar

Palm Leaf Rag

by Scott Joplin

The best way to get to knowing any bunch
of people is to go and listen to their music.
Woody Guthrie

Ragtime Cowboy Joe

Words and Music by Lewis F. Muir,
Grant Clark and Maurice Abrahams

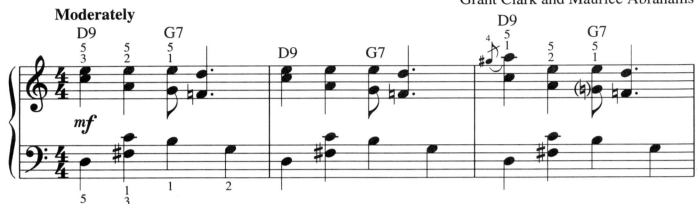

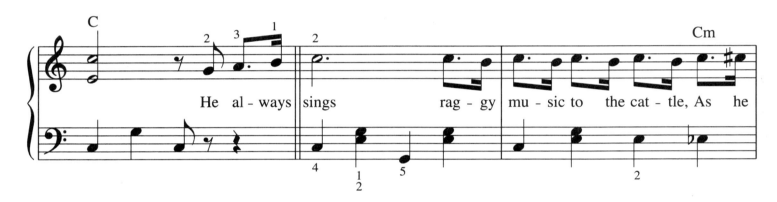

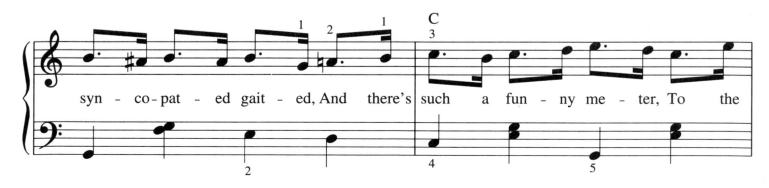

*What is best in music is not
to be found in the notes.*
Gustav Mahler

RECITAL SOLO

Changing Times

by Frank Metis

Boogie waltz (as before)

*Growth is more important
to me than talent.*
  Painter Susan Rothenberg

THE CREATIVE CORNER! Add to the existing right hand Melody a left hand Boogie accompaniment, based either on the suggested rhythm (in small cue notes), or on rhythm figurations of your own choosing. Write in the left hand in pencil. Also, select a suitable title.

Title: _____

Bright boogie

by _____